I'm a
SUPER
SECRET

FIGHTER

AUTUMN
PUBLISHING

I have a secret that nobody knows...

... I'm a Super Secret Germ Fighter!

I'm a SUPER SECRET GERM FIGHTER

AUTUMN
PUBLISHING

Published in 2022
First published in the UK by Autumn Publishing
An imprint of Igloo Books Ltd
Cottage Farm, NN6 0BJ, UK
Owned by Bonnier Books
Sveavägen 56, Stockholm, Sweden
www.autumnpublishing.co.uk

0122 001
2 4 6 8 10 9 7 5 3 1
ISBN 978-1-80022-272-4

Illustrated by Purificación Hernández
Written by Wednesday Jones

Designed by Lee Italiano
Edited by Suzanne Fossey

Printed and manufactured in China

After I've been to the toilet and whenever I'm about to eat, I **wash** my hands using **lots** of **soap**. I **scrub away** and watch the germs swirl down the drain.

Fruit and veggies contain lots of special vitamins that help my body fight the germs.

They keep me healthy, so I try to eat as many as I can.

Even the yucky ones...

Being **active** helps **boost** my Super-Secret Germ Fighter immune system, so my body can fight off germs.

I move **so fast** that germs **can't keep up** with me.

I try not to bite my fingernails or suck my thumbs, especially after playing outside at the park. I use special Germ Fighter sanitiser to keep my hands clean.

I don't share drinks with other people because we might pass germs onto each other. Sometimes germs come from even the nicest of places.

Germs are really sneaky, but I am sneakier.

I brush my teeth every morning and every night. That way, they can't creep in when I'm not looking.

I can fight germs better when my body is well rested, so I try to get lots of sleep. That way, I can wake up ready to fight germs all over again.

If one of my friends
gets sick, I'll give them
some space.

I don't have to ignore them,
but I won't hug them again
until they're better.

Sometimes I have to go and see the doctor. They might give me a little injection to super-charge my body's germ-fighting powers. Or, if I'm sick, they might give me medicine to make me better.

If the germs do somehow make me sick, I'll sneeze and cough into my elbow, or into a tissue and then put it in the bin.

Here you go.

If I leave them all over the place and someone else touches them, they might get sick too.

THE HYGIENE HERO CHECKLIST

Bacteria and viruses are tiny, tiny creatures so small that we cannot see them without a microscope. Some of them are good and help our bodies to stay healthy, but some are bad and can make us sick. The bad ones are called germs. Germs are so sneaky that they can creep into our bodies without being noticed.

One of the best ways to beat germs is to **wash your hands** often. Do these **five steps** every time you wash your hands to **defeat those pesky germs**.

Wet your hands using running water.

Put a little bit of soap in the palm of your hand.

Rub your hands together for at least 20 seconds.
Don't forget to wash the backs of your hands, in between your fingers and around your nails.

Wash off all the soap and turn off the tap.

Dry your hands with a clean towel.